Sometimes..

(101 DAYS OF HEALING THROUGH WORDS)

-VISHAKHA JAIN-

Disclaimer:
This book is offered as a reflection of personal experiences and
perspectives. It is not a substitute for professional help.
If you are experiencing emotional distress or mental health
challenges, please reach out to a licensed professional or support
service. Your well-being matters most.

For more information, contact:
(hello@thespiritualabode.com)

ISBN: 978-1-0694394-0-6

SOMETIMES..

To all the painful life lessons and rock bottoms
that brought out the writer in me.

P.S. Now I know everything happens for a reason

VISHAKHA JAIN

For those who are learning to heal,
one day at a time.

POV:
"Some healing is loud, but most of it happens in silence."

Sometimes, healing comes in the quiet moments, when you least expect it. In the *stillness*, you find the *answers* you've been searching for, and in the silence, you find the *peace* you've been craving for.

...Day 1

"Boundaries are a form of self-love."

Sometimes, the most loving thing you can do for yourself is set boundaries. Not everyone deserves access to your energy. And not everyone will understand your healing. But you don't have to explain your peace to those who only know you through your pain. The version of you that's choosing themselves might scare them. That's okay.

Choose you anyway.

...Day 2

"Love should fill you, not drain you."

SOMETIMES..

Sometimes, you give until there's nothing left. You pour every drop of yourself into people who never stop to *refill you*. But love isn't about *running on empty*, it's about balance. You deserve someone who not only drinks from your cup but also makes sure your cup is *full* too.

...Day 3

"Some wounds don't leave scars,
just lessons."

SOMETIMES..

Sometimes, healing makes you realize that you deserve better – *better treatment, a better relationship, and a better life.* However, the only reason you're holding onto the old is because it has become your comfort zone. Remember, magic happens when you decide that *enough is enough* and take action to step away from what's not serving *you* and your *higher self.*

...Day 4

"Your peace is non-negotiable."

Sometimes, healing involves creating healthy boundaries. It requires making the decision to *delete, unfollow, unfriend, block, remove, and detach* yourself from anyone and anything that deprives you of *love, joy, and happiness* because nothing is worth more than your inner peace. It's about deciding not to surround yourself with people who fail to acknowledge and appreciate your *worth*, your *love*, your *value*, and the support you offer.

...Day 5

"Choose distance over disrespect."
#DailyReminder

Sometimes, healing makes you realize that the only answer to disrespect, betrayal, or any negative situation is *distance*. You choose to walk away because you no longer want to react, argue, or fight to prove your point. Instead, you simply prefer to remove yourself from the conversation and the situation that affects your *peace of mind*.

...Day 6

VISHAKHA JAIN

"Love should not feel like a battlefield."

Sometimes, you have to realize that what isn't meant for

you will never stay in your life, regardless of convincing,
begging, or ultimatums. Then why beg, why chase, why
convince them to pick you, choose you, love you?
You are better than this.
Let them go!

...Day 7

"*True love will make your heart beat again, feel again, and love again.*"

Sometimes, love finds you when you least expect it. It slowly enters through the cracks and glues the pieces of your heart back together to make it *whole* again, to *beat* again, to *feel* again, and to love again. Sometimes this healing love comes from someone else; sometimes, that someone is **you**.

...Day 8

"What if everything I went through was shaping me?"

Sometimes, strength doesn't look like holding it together. It looks like breaking down and still choosing to get back up the next day.

...Day 9

"Healing begins when you accept what's broken."

SOMETIMES..

Sometimes, healing begins with *acceptance*,

Accepting that there are parts of you still carrying pain,

and a willingness to do whatever it takes to *heal*.

...Day 10

"The universe only gives when you're ready to receive."

Sometimes, the universe tests you before it blesses you, to see if you have healed, grown, and learned your lessons. So, stay strong, don't lower your worth, and especially don't go back to the old patterns.

Show the universe *you're ready for your blessings*!

...Day 11

"*Choose someone out of love, not because you are scared of being alone.*"

Sometimes, you need to learn the difference between being lonely and being alone. Being 'alone' is a physical state, while being 'lonely' is a state of mind. Don't settle for the wrong person just because you feel lonely.

Remember, unless you learn to be comfortable being alone, you'll never know if you're choosing someone out of *love* or *loneliness.*

...Day 12

"You deserve to be seen, heard, and valued."

Sometimes, you stay silent to keep the peace, even when it's breaking you inside. But peace that comes at the cost of your voice isn't peace, it's self-abandonment. You deserve to be *heard, seen, respected, and valued.*

...Day 13

"Crying is not a weakness; it's a release."

SOMETIMES..

Sometimes, it's *okay to cry*. It's okay to feel all the feels, to ugly cry, to be vulnerable, to let down your walls, and to reach out for a shoulder to lean on.

It's about *accepting* that what you are feeling, whether big or small, is valid too, and you don't have to put on a happy face all the time!

...Day 14

"It's beautiful being a woman."

SOMETIMES..

Sometimes, it's hard to be a woman,
to give all you have and get breadcrumbs in return.

Sometimes it's hard to believe in old-school love,
when everyone around you is swiping left.

Sometimes it's hard to love someone
who doesn't understand your silence.

Yes, sometimes it's hard to be a woman,
when you give all your love to one man.

But sometimes it's *beautiful to be a woman*,
because you love, fight, and grow in ways only you can
understand.

...Day 15

*"The pain that breaks you
is the same pain that
makes you stronger."*

SOMETIMES..

Sometimes, you'll find that the moments that *break you* are the same moments that *make you*. You won't see it at first, the cracks in your heart seem too wide, the pain too deep. But it's in those spaces, in the dark corners where you think hope no longer exists, that your resilience takes root. And from there, you'll grow into someone you never thought you could be.

...Day 16

VISHAKHA JAIN

"You matter; you matter a lot. Feel it, believe it."

Sometimes, you have to remind yourself that 'You matter.'
It doesn't matter how broken, shattered, worthless, helpless,
or hopeless you feel. You matter. *You matter a lot.*

...Day 17

"You deserve the same love you give."

SOMETIMES..

Sometimes, you spend so much time taking care of others that you forget you need care too. You pour your heart out for everyone else, but what about you?
You deserve the same love and attention you give so freely.
Remember, you matter just as much.

...Day 18

"Trust the universe; believe your dreams will manifest one day or maybe someday in divine timing."

Sometimes, you have to be so confident in the universe's plan that you no longer get angry, upset, or cry, and don't lose hope when things don't go your way.

Remember, successful manifestation requires absolute trust in the Universe.

...Day 19

"People don't trigger you,
they trigger your triggers.
#HealYourTriggers"

Sometimes, healing makes you realize that the people who trigger negative emotions are just messengers-messengers for the *unhealed parts of you* that still need more *healing.*

...Day 20

"Rest is necessity, not a luxury."

Sometimes, you just need to take a step back and rest.

You've been carrying so much for so long that you forget what it feels like to breathe.

Rest isn't a *reward*, it's a *necessity*.

You don't have to earn it; you deserve it just as you are.

...Day 21

"*Let go of control and trust the process.*"

SOMETIMES..

Sometimes, you just need to let go of control, go with the flow, and allow things to unfold naturally. This requires releasing the urge to force people, relationships, or situations to go your way. It's about trusting that, regardless of the outcome, things are unfolding in ways beyond your human understanding.

Trust that the Universe is always working in your favor.

Affirm: Everything always works out for me!

...Day 22

"The beauty is in the present moment."

SOMETIMES..

Sometimes, life is about being in the present;
not crying about the past or worrying about the future.
Simply, *here and now*:
The butterfly, the bumblebee, the shape of the cloud, the
baby's laughter, the scent after the first fresh rain, the
warmth of sunlight on your skin, your favorite song playing
in a loop, and a warm hug from your mother.

...Day 23

"Self-respect is the ultimate form of self-love."

Sometimes, your self-respect has to be stronger than your emotions—or rather, most of the time. It's about *choosing silence* when all you want to send is a long paragraph. It's about choosing *distance over disrespect* and walking away when all you want is to fight for answers. It's about choosing to love yourself instead of begging for the love you should have never had to question.

...Day 24

"She deserves to be seen, heard, and valued."

Sometimes, she just wants to feel seen and heard.

When someone listens to her without interrupting, thinks about her feelings when making decisions, pays attention to small details about what she likes and needs, and does kind things to show they care, it means the world to her.

In those moments, she feels truly *valued* and *loved*.

...Day 25

VISHAKHA JAIN

"Step up, glow up, and claim what's yours."

SOMETIMES..

Sometimes, healing is all about trusting your intuition and following what your heart desires, even if it means taking massive risks, or simply stepping out of your *comfort zone*. It may seem scary, but you are worth more than what you are settling for, my love.

Step up, be bold, and claim what is already *YOURS*!

...Day 26

#Heal #Glow #Grow

Sometimes, the most healing thing you can do is allow
yourself to feel it all—the pain, the joy, the fear, the love.
You don't have to numb it or push it away.
Let yourself feel every part of it. *Heal, grow,* and *glow.*
And when it all passes, you'll still be standing, stronger than
before.

...Day 27

"You've cried in silence, fought your battles alone,
but you're still here. That's resilience."

Sometimes, the strongest people are those who love despite the scars, who cry silent tears—in the closet, in the shower, in the rain, when no one's watching—and fight battles only they know exist, all while carrying a *heart* that still finds a way to *hope*.

...Day 28

"Heal, believe, and rise like a phoenix."
#RootingForYou

SOMETIMES..

Sometimes, you have to pick yourself up from the ground, dust off your clothes, let go of past traumas, and believe you can *heal* and *fly* to a new mental space.
A place where your mind is powerful, your thoughts shape your reality, manifestation is real, and there is only love and happiness, with no space for fears and pain.

...Day 29

"Your feelings matter too, and it's okay to put yourself first."

SOMETIMES..

Sometimes, you neglect your own feelings and emotions
and put others first because you're scared of hurting their
feelings. Until one day, you really get hurt and realize you are
also human and your feelings and emotions matter too.
You too deserve to be *prioritized*, the way you have been
prioritizing others.

...Day 30

"Stop chasing people who don't value you."

Sometimes, self-love is all about you.

You need to stop focusing on people who aren't focused on you, stop worrying about people who aren't worried about you, and stop prioritizing people when they aren't *prioritizing you.*

...Day 31

"Choose respect, peace, and self-respect over anything that drains your energy."

Sometimes, you have to choose your battles:

choose respect over love, choose peace over drama,

choose distance over disrespect, and above all,

choose *self-respect* over *anxious attachment* that

you call *love*.

...*Day 32*

"Letting go is the first step to finding yourself."

SOMETIMES..

Sometimes, you hold on to relationships, friendships, and situations that no longer serve you because you're scared of being alone. But eventually, you realize that holding on hurts more than letting go.
And the day you decide to let go, you end up *finding yourself.*

...Day 33

"The universe tests you before it blesses you."

SOMETIMES..

Sometimes, the universe tests your commitment and
patience, not because you weren't ready the first time
around, but simply because the universe has been preparing
you to receive way beyond what you have been asking,
hoping, and praying for.
Stay strong and keep holding on; your life is about to become
magical beyond your wildest dreams.

...Day 34

VISHAKHA JAIN

"Saying yes to yourself is the first step to self-love."

SOMETIMES..

Sometimes, you say yes to others when every part of you is screaming no, because you don't want to disappoint or hurt anyone. But then you realize that by constantly saying yes to them, you've been saying no to yourself.
And it's time to start choosing *you*.

...Day 35

"Healing is finding balance between the strength to hold on and the courage to let go."

Sometimes, healing isn't about feeling privileged,

cutting people out of your life, or giving up on them while
building steel walls around your heart.
Healing also involves being *kind, compassionate,* and
forgiving, having the ability to break down your own walls,
and accepting that others are humans too.
Remember, healing is about finding the balance of when to
hold on and *fight* for it, and when to *release* and *let go.*

...Day 36

"Mistakes are always life lessons, not failures."

Sometimes, we all make mistakes.

You are not any less for making them; in fact, you are more because you have learned from them.

Remember, mistakes do not break you apart; instead, they provide you with an opportunity to rebuild yourself.

...Day 37

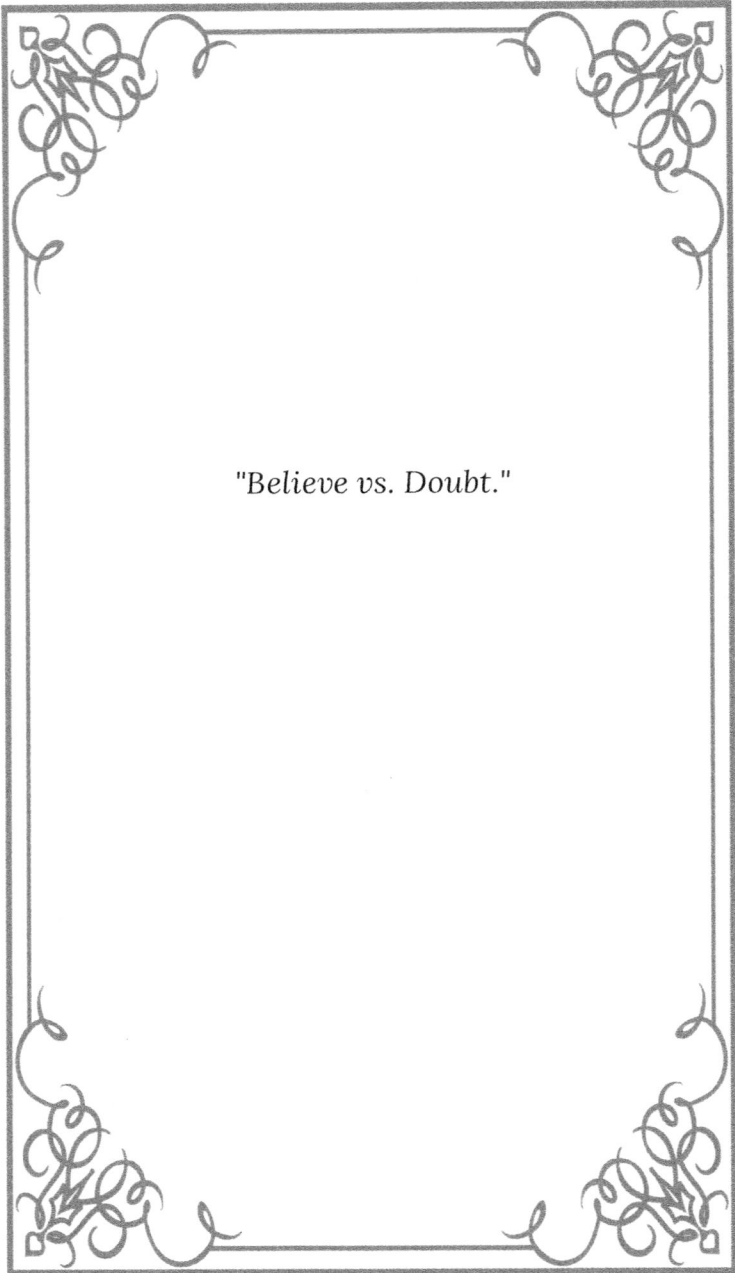

"Believe vs. Doubt."

Sometimes, it's hard to stay strong when one part of you just wants to give up, yet a tiny part of you still believes that your dreams will come true.

It's a constant battle between *belief vs doubt.*

But *remember*, the universe has a way of surprising us when we least expect it.

...Day 38

"Rewrite a new story."

SOMETIMES..

Sometimes, you have to remind yourself that trauma may
have left you broken with scars in the past,
but healing helps you to heal your scars,
rewrite a new story with a new *beginning*, and a new *ending*.

...*Day 39*

"When they're unsure,
it's time to choose yourself."

Sometimes, healing is needed to make you realize you are way too good for someone to be unsure of you.
If they fail to recognize your worth, it's not a reflection of you lacking, *it's a reminder that you deserve more.*

...Day 40

"You deserve better than what you're settling for,
just because it's familiar."

SOMETIMES..

Sometimes, you cling to the idea of how things were

supposed to be, and it hurts to let go of that vision.

It's hard to release the control you thought you had.

But healing begins when you stop asking *why me?*

And start saying *what's next?*

Let go of the life you imagined to make space for the one

that's waiting for you, because the universe didn't bring you

this far to settle for less than you deserve.

...Day 41

"Your scars will one day be your story of strength
and resilience."

Sometimes, you have to remember that your scars may hurt really bad right now, but these will make great stories full of wisdom about *healing, resilience*, and *strength* and how you overcome them to be shared with your future generations.

...Day 42

"Sometimes, life falls apart
to make space for something better."

SOMETIMES..

Sometimes, life gets in the way.

You think you have it all together, but suddenly things fall apart. You lose the love of your life, your business fails, you lose your job, and all your money is gone. It may feel like the end of the world, hitting rock bottom.

But sometimes, our lives need to be completely shaken up, rearranged, and transformed to guide us to our true *destiny*, our *soul path*, and our *soulmate*.

...Day 43

"Are you the main character of your own story?"

SOMETIMES..

Sometimes, healing is all about finding yourself and recognizing your true self-worth.
It involves releasing and letting go of the past, remembering who the f**k you really are, and claiming your right to be the *main character* of your own beautiful *story*!

...Day 44

"Putting yourself first is the most powerful choice you can make."

Sometimes, you find yourself bending over backwards for
those who wouldn't lift a finger for you.
But one day, through healing, you'll *rise*,
choosing to put yourself first and realizing how powerful it
feels to no longer shrink for anyone.

...Day 45

VISHAKHA JAIN

"Is it love if it brings confusion?"

SOMETIMES..

Sometimes, you have to remember that the right one will
always bring you clarity, safety, and security, and
the wrong one will bring confusion, love-bombing,
gaslighting, and a loss of self.
So, heal and choose love that *writes your story*,
not erases your chapters.

...Day 46

VISHAKHA JAIN

"Break the pattern, or you'll repeat the past."

Sometimes, detaching and letting go of the person who consistently hurt you in the past isn't enough; you must also let go of the version of you who allowed this to continue, letting this happen to you for as long as it did.
Otherwise, you'll end up attracting the same situationship and the *same person*, but in a *different body*.

...Day 47

"Sometimes, detours take you exactly where you need to go."

Sometimes, you make the wrong choices to reach the right place. Those choices end up being your biggest lessons- the catalyst for your healing, that ultimately leads you to the right path.

...Day 48

"Energy is precious, spend it wisely."

Sometimes, choosing yourself feels selfish, but it's the bravest thing you can do. You don't owe anyone your time, your energy, or your heart, especially if it costs you your peace.

In choosing yourself, you find your freedom.

...Day 49

"She is me..."

Sometimes, the strongest women walk away with tears in their eyes—not because they're weak, but because they're brave enough to choose *peace over pain*.

They leave behind what no longer serves them, even when it breaks their heart, because they know that staying would mean losing pieces of themselves, they can never get back.

...Day 50

"Forgive yourself the way you forgive others."

Sometimes, the hardest person to forgive is yourself.

You replay the mistakes, the choices, the moments you wish you could take back. But healing means offering yourself the same grace, compassion, and kindness you give so freely to others.

...Day 51

"#PerfectlyImperfect"

Sometimes, healing means not chasing the dream of being 'Perfect'- perfect body, perfect bank balance, perfect job, perfect relationship.

It's about accepting that you are *perfect just the way you are*.

Loving this perfectly imperfect version of yourself!

...Day 52

"You are healing for yourself, it's your journey."

Sometimes, healing means accepting that not everyone will understand your journey, and that's okay.
You're not healing for *them*; you're healing for *you*.
Let their opinions fade, and don't let their limited mindset interfere with your progress.
Keep the focus on yourself—because, let's be real, your healing never needed their approval in the first place.

...Day 53

"Believe that love will come when you're ready to receive it."

SOMETIMES..

Sometimes, you have to believe that the perfect person for you is out there and that you have worked through your old traumas and blocks, and are *open* and *ready* to receive their presence in your life.

...Day 54

"*Healing is a journey, not a destination.*"

Sometimes, healing is messy.

It's not linear, and it doesn't happen overnight.
There are setbacks, relapses, and days when you feel like giving up. But every step forward, no matter how small, is progress. And one day, you'll look back and see just how far you've come.

...Day 55

"Let them go if they don't align with your energy."

Sometimes, healing requires setting healthy boundaries and *being okay with losing people* who do not align with your current vibrational energy.

It's not about cutting people off; it's about making space for those who truly support and uplift you.

...Day 56

"You've survived what was meant to break you—
now, it's your time to shine."

SOMETIMES..

Sometimes, you have to pat yourself on the back and be
super proud of yourself for surviving the battles you've never
told anyone about, and for staying strong even when you felt
like giving up.
Your moment to shine is here, and life is going to be so
beautiful and *magical.*

...Day 57

VISHAKHA JAIN

"BeYOUtiful"

SOMETIMES..

Sometimes, you fail to realize how special you are and the happiness you bring into other people's lives because you are too busy criticizing the extra 20 pounds, the pimple on your skin, the way you dress, the way you talk, and the way you walk.

Remember, the things you constantly criticize about make you 'YOU,' and you are *beautiful*!

...Day 58

"Your worth is non-negotiable."

Sometimes, the most healing thing you can do is recognize that you deserve more—more love, more respect, more peace. And once you realize that, don't be afraid to ask for it. Your worth is *non-negotiable*.

...Day 59

VISHAKHA JAIN

"Let's normalize taking accountability for our own
healing."

Sometimes, you need to stop blaming your kismet, your karma, your husband, boyfriend, mother, father, children, uncles, and aunts. Take *responsibility* for your own healing.

Remember, what has happened has happened.
Now you have two choices: either keep up with the blame game and stay stuck, or heal and create a new life full of love and laughter.
The choice is really *yours*.

...Day 60

"Trust that time will reveal your soul path."

Sometimes, you got to go where your heart wants to go. Maybe to a place far away or maybe someplace closer to home. Trust that wherever you go, time will reveal your *destiny* when it's the *divine time*.

...Day 61

"You're a prized possession, accept it, behave like it."

Sometimes, you have to heal and wait for someone who values you. It's okay to think you're too good for some people. Not everyone deserves to have you in their life because now,
you're no longer a doormat- you're a *prized possession*!

...Day 62

"Be *unapologetically* YOU."

Sometimes, you need to be *unapologetic*.

Be unapologetic for taking too much space, for being too loud, for being overly sensitive and emotional, for being different.

Remember, you are "YOU" and your beauty is in being authentically "BeYOUtiful".

...Day 63

"It's better to be alone than to feel alone in a relationship."

Sometimes, you hold on to toxic relationships beyond their
expiration date because you're afraid of being alone.
But there's more loneliness in being with someone who
doesn't value you. It's better to be *happy alone* than to lie
awake in bed *feeling alone in a relationship*.

...*Day 64*

"*You are worth more than being someone's 'maybe.'*"

Sometimes, the real lesson we need to learn is *recognizing*
and *acknowledging* that if someone truly wants to be in your
life or prioritize you, they will make the effort and take the
necessary actions to show it—to you and to others.
It's about loving yourself enough to realize that you are
worth more than settling for 'potential' or
being someone's 'maybe.'

...Day 65

"You deserve love that comes naturally, not
something you have to teach."

Sometimes, the more you heal, the more you realize that you don't need to teach someone how to love you or how to treat you better.

Instead, you deserve someone who makes you feel *safe, seen, loved, understood, appreciated,* and *supported.*

...Day 66

"The hardest moments often lead to the greatest growth."

Sometimes, the struggles, failures, and rock bottoms are important because they change you, making you into the person you are today.
They teach you lessons that no amount of success would have been able to otherwise.
Remember, you're not just surviving the tough times; you're thriving because of them.

...Day 67

"Even the strongest need moments of vulnerability."
#BeingHuman

Sometimes, the ones who seem the strongest are the ones who feel the most alone.

They carry the weight of the world in silence, hoping no one notices how much they're hurting.

But remember, at times, even the *strongest need someone to lean on.*

...Day 68

"Rise from the ashes, own your power, and become unstoppable."
#Heal #Grow #Rise

Sometimes, you have to realize that healing isn't all a bed

of roses, or a warm, fuzzy blanket and a cup of honey on a

cozy winter morning.

Healing is scary; it's painful and uncomfortable.

It will first break you and shake you up inside out.

Then, piece by piece, it will build you back up like a phoenix

rising from the ashes, creating a new you who is *stronger*,

more *confident*, and more in love with your own mind, body,

and soul. Someone who knows what they *want* and what

they truly *deserve*.

...Day 69

"Love should always make sense in the present moment."

SOMETIMES..

Sometimes, you need to stop pretending to be in love
because it makes sense to other people.
Stop holding onto love because it might make sense in the
future. Instead, stay in love and hold onto love because it
makes sense in the *present*.
Love should always make sense NOW!

...Day 70

"Affirm: I am open and ready to receive the love I truly deserve. I release all fears as I open my heart to love again."

Sometimes, healing requires courage to break down the walls and trust someone with your heart again- to love again. The thought may seem scary because you have been badly hurt in the past and you may feel like running away instead of facing your fears but *remember*, everyone deserves to find their special someone their one true love.
And so do you!

...Day 71

Affirm: "I am beautiful, I am worthy and enough just the way I am!"

Sometimes, healing is realizing that what other people think about your body, weight, skin, color, or height isn't the real problem. The true problem and it's solution lies in how you feel about yourself.

Ask yourself, do you feel beautiful, sexy, intelligent, and, most importantly, do you feel *worthy* and *enough* just the way you are?

...Day 72

"Be enough for yourself first."

Sometimes, you're so busy being everything for everyone else that you forget you can't be everything to everyone. You realize that in trying to be enough for others, you've forgotten to be *enough for yourself*.

...Day 73

"You don't owe anyone an explanation–choose your peace."

Sometimes, healing involves deciding who deserves your explanation, learning not to seek external validation, and avoiding wasting your energy on invalid justifications.

...Day 74

Affirm: "My feelings are valid, and I deserve to take up space to grow and thrive."

Sometimes, you need to remind yourself that your feelings are valid. You're allowed to take up space, to feel deeply, and to put yourself first. Your *needs* and *emotions* are just as important as anyone else's.

...Day 75

"Forgiveness is a gift you give yourself."

SOMETIMES..

Sometimes, healing comes when you finally forgive yourself. Not just for what you've done, but for what you didn't know at the time. For the choices you made when you were just trying to survive.

Forgiveness isn't for them—it's for *you.*

...Day 76

"*Forgive the person, the situation, and the pain—but never forget the lesson.*"

Sometimes, healing isn't about moving on; it's about moving forward, carrying the lessons, the strength, and the resilience you gained from the pain, but leaving the hurt behind. It's about forgiving, not forgetting. Forgiving the people and situations but never forgetting the lessons.

...Day 77

"You are human at the end of the day."

SOMETIMES..

Sometimes, you convince yourself that you're okay, that
you can handle it all, that you don't need anyone's help.
But then it hits you, you deserve support, you deserve to be
taken care of, and you deserve to rest.
Above all, you *deserve to be loved* for who you are.

...Day 78

"Life is all about living for the moments that take your breath away."

Sometimes, you are forced to live in the moment, neither in the future nor in the past, and sometimes, you end up finding that one moment that takes your breath away and makes living worthwhile.

...Day 79

"Heal your inner child to heal your relationships."

SOMETIMES..

Sometimes, your unaddressed and unresolved inner child wounds impact on how you handle relationships, especially when you're very close to someone.

It's more likely that you'll encounter repeated patterns, trust issues, a need for constant validation, and a consistent need for 'I love you's' before hanging up the call, feelings of insecurity and lack of safety, frequent arguments, or difficulty staying calm.

...Day 80

"What's meant for you, won't pass you by."

Sometimes, the biggest battle is the one between what you know in your head and what you feel in your heart.

Your head says to move on, but your heart says to give it just one more try.

Remember, what's meant for you won't pass you by, so why not focus on self-healing in the meantime.

...Day 81

VISHAKHA JAIN

*"Be okay with being alone and bored.
#DopamineDetox"*

Sometimes, healing is about being comfortable with silence and stillness, feeling happy in your own company, getting used to being alone, and accepting moments of boredom rather than spending hours mindlessly scrolling through the internet, watching too much Netflix, or indulging in random online shopping.

Remember, it's your healing era, and it's time to learn to be still enough to listen to your body, your mind, and your higher self.

...Day 82

"Feel, break, rise, and rebuild."

Sometimes, the hardest part of healing is letting go of the idea that you need to be strong all the time.
Real healing happens when you allow yourself to *feel*, to *break*, and to *rebuild* at your own *pace*.

...Day 83

"Growth means leaving behind what no longer serves you."

Sometimes, it's not that you've changed too much, it's that you've grown. And with growth comes the realization that not everyone can come with you.
It's okay to outgrow *people, places,* and *things* that no longer serve you.

...Day 84

"Strength is discovered when you have no choice but to keep going."

SOMETIMES..

Sometimes, you don't know how strong you are until you have no choice but to be.
One day, you'll look back on this moment and see how far you've come, realizing it was worth every tear,
every sleepless night, and every moment you felt utterly helpless and alone.

...Day 85

"Not everyone who enters your life is meant to stay,
but they all end up teaching you something."

Sometimes, we learn that life isn't always like a beautiful

story. Not everyone we feel a strong connection with is
meant to be with us forever.
Sometimes, people enter our lives to show us how to love,
while others teach us how not to settle or shrink ourselves.
It's okay if people leave because the *lessons* they teach us stay
with us, and that's what's important.

...Day 86

"You deserve effort, not excuses."

SOMETIMES..

Sometimes, you have to heal and love yourself so fiercely that, once you start dating and someone tells you they were too busy to text you, you can look them right in the eyes and say, 'I believe you, but I'm not going to keep you.'

Remember, relationships built on mutual effort and reciprocation are the ones that last the longest.

...Day 87

VISHAKHA JAIN

"*You are the author of your own story.*"

Sometimes, it's easy to forget that you are the author of
your own life. You get so caught up in playing the role of
caretaker, friend, or partner that you forget to write yourself
into the story.
But you are the most important character,
don't leave yourself behind.

...Day 88

"It's all about being happy within, without relying on the external factors."

Sometimes, healing makes you realize that instead of filling the void that you feel inside of you with Amazon shopping, binge-eating, and random dating, maybe all it ever needed was self-love and being happy with *who* you are, *where* you are, and *what all* you already *have*.

...Day 89

"No more settling for breadcrumbs. Not anymore."

Sometimes, the love you give others is the love you
desperately crave for yourself. You pour your heart into
everyone else, hoping someone will pour back into you.
But the truth is, no one can love you the way you can love
yourself. So why not *love yourself so fiercely* that you teach
others how you deserve to be loved?
Show them you deserve so much more than the bare
minimum and that you won't settle for breadcrumbs.
Not anymore.

...Day 90

"The best connections don't need words, just you and their presence."

Sometimes, you crave a relationship where the best
conversations happen in silence.
It's like words aren't needed-just the company, the
understanding, and the shared moments.

...Day 91

"Respect, kindness, and love
are not luxuries—they're
the bare minimum."

Sometimes, you convince yourself that you're asking for too much. But respect, kindness, time, and real love aren't luxuries, they're the bare minimum.

Don't settle for less than you deserve just because you were never taught self-worth. It's time to remind yourself that you are worthy of everything, *exactly as you are.*

...Day 92

"Ask yourself, am I happy?"

SOMETIMES..

Sometimes, healing makes us realize that being single and
being in a relationship maybe are two ends of the same
spectrum, but they do have a common denominator,
and that denominator is your level of happiness.
It doesn't matter which side you are on;
what matters is how *happy* you really are.

...Day 93

"Change your paradigm to transform your life."

Sometimes, you have to fight to *break the cycle* you are trapped in. Just because it's the only option and reality you have ever seen and known, doesn't mean it's the only one you are destined to experience forever.

...Day 94

"Forgive the past, but remember the lessons."

Sometimes, healing is all about *forgiving* but not *forgetting*:
forgiving the person, the situation, the pain, and the trauma,
while never forgetting the lessons you've learned.
Keep these lessons as reminders that you have *grown* and
you don't have to go through the same pattern again.

...Day 95

"You are whole and complete just as you are."

SOMETIMES..

Sometimes, you don't need someone to complete you;
instead, you just need someone to accept you as you really
are, *no strings attached.*

...Day 96

VISHAKHA JAIN

"Broken yet Beautiful"

Sometimes, you look at your reflection and only see what's wrong. But the flaws you pick apart are the very things that make you human, real, and worthy.
Stop seeing yourself through the eyes of someone who viewed you through the filters of their own wounds and insecurities, and start seeing yourself through the eyes of real, pure, authentic love.
You've always been *perfectly imperfect* and beautifully enough-you just need to believe it.

...Day 97

"True strength is discovered when you're pushed to your breaking point."

SOMETIMES..

Sometimes, you don't realize how strong you are until life gives you no other choice. In those moments, you find a strength you never knew existed. And it's in those moments that you realize you are capable of surviving even the hardest battles.

...Day 98

"*Let go and let them go.*"

Sometimes, the greatest act of love you can give yourself is permission to let go. To release the past, the pain, and the weight of what no longer serves you.
Leave the baggage behind, and step forward lighter, stronger, and finally free to *welcome what's really meant for you.*

...Day 99

"Letting go isn't weakness; it's strength in choosing yourself."

SOMETIMES..

Sometimes, you feel drained because you've been holding
the weight of expectations, generational wounds, and
unspoken burdens that were never truly yours to bear.
It's time to heal, to let go, and
to set yourself *free, be free, feel free.*
Letting go doesn't mean you're weak.
It means you're finally strong enough to choose yourself.

...Day 100

"The cycle only ends when you choose your peace over their empty promises. Break the pattern, heal, and reclaim your life."

I'm rooting for you every step of the way.

Sometimes, you let people back in, hoping it will be
different this time. But the truth is, patterns don't lie, and
promises without actions are just words.
The cycle only ends when you decide your peace is worth
more than their *empty apologies.*
Remember, breaking the pattern is the only way to truly heal
and stop reliving the same pain over and over again.

...Day 101

Sometimes, the healing journey is just the beginning of finding your true self.

About The Author

Vishakha Jain is a Canadian author whose roots trace back to India. She discovered her passion for writing later in life and now focuses on themes like self-love, self-worth, and emotional healing.

Her words are inspired by the quiet strength it takes to choose yourself, over and over again.

You can find her work here:

instagram.com/thespiritualabode
facebook.com/thespiritualabode
tiktok.com/@thespiritualabode
threads.net/@thespiritualabode
pinterest.com/thespiritualabode/

VISHAKHA JAIN

Printed in Dunstable, United Kingdom

71509285R00122